U.S. Department of Commerce
National Institute of Standards and Technology

Office of Applied Economics
Building and Fire Research Laboratory
Gaithersburg, MD 20899

Guidelines for Planning and Development of Software for Buildings and Building Systems

Priya D. Lavappa

Sponsored by:
National Institute of Standards and Technology
Building and Fire Research Laboratory

June 2008

U.S. DEPARTMENT OF COMMERCE
Carlos M. Gutierrez, Secretary

NATIONAL INSTITUTE OF STANDARDS AND TECHNOLOGY
James Turner, Deputy Director

Abstract

From inception to completion, software development projects need structure and organization so that good quality, user-friendly software is produced on time and within budget. The structured approach presented in this paper helps achieve those goals.

The System Development Life Cycle (SDLC) is a conceptual model for software development that divides up the process into different phases. Each phase has a distinct role to play in the development life cycle, and is a building block for the next phase. There are many SDLC models, each emphasizing different aspects of the life-cycle. Implementing a structured approach requires selecting a model and utilizing it through out the development life cycle.

This paper selects a Waterfall model for planning and executing a software project; describes the steps each research team member takes, by project phase, in the development of the software product; provides a one-page summary of those steps for making a checklist of team progress; provides a blank and case illustration template for each team member to fill out in providing requirements or specifications of the software and provides a blank project schedule template for documenting the tasks required to implement the software project design.

Following a structured process enables software development projects to be organized and have a clear path to completion. Implementing a structured process is crucial for developing good quality software in an efficient manner.

Keywords: System Development Life Cycle, Waterfall model, software project management, software development, software requirements template.

Preface

This paper describes the steps in the software development process, knowledge of which is useful to organize and structure software development projects. Structuring a software development project from inception provides a clear path to completion. This set of guidelines provides a software development team with a progression of steps to conceive code, test, revise, and publish software applications that will best satisfy clients' software needs. Following these steps will clarify the respective roles for a software development team, show how their tasks fit together in a time schedule, and contribute to an on-time, successful, within budget software product. These steps have been used by the author on numerous software development projects, both large and small, using an assortment of technologies. These projects have focused on various topics including: economics, biological sciences, insurance, taxation, and accounting. The staff members of the Office of Applied Economics in the Building and Fire Research Laboratory at the National Institute of Standards and Technology use these guidelines and templates in their software development projects.

Disclaimer: Certain trade names and company products are mentioned in the text in order to adequately specify the technical procedures and equipment used. In no case does such identification imply recommendation or endorsement by the National Institute of Standards and Technology, nor does it imply that the products are necessarily the best available for the purpose.

Acknowledgments

The author would like to thank all those who helped bring this paper to fruition. I would like to thank Dr. Robert Chapman, Ms. Barbara Lippiattt, and Dr. Harold Marshall, of the Office of Applied Economics (OAE), for all of their insightful suggestions.

Contents

List of Acronyms

BEES	Building for Environmental and Economic Sustainability
BusiBEES	Business Case for Sustainability
BFRL	Building and Fire Research Laboratory
DLL	Dynamic Link Library
EPA	Environmental Protection Agency
LCA	Life-Cycle Assessment
LCC	Life-Cycle Cost
NIST	National Institute of Standards and Technology
OAE	Office of Applied Economics
OMB	Office of Management and Budget
PDF	Portable Document Format
SDLC	System Development Life Cycle

1   Introduction

1.1   Background

Understanding the nature of a research problem as defined by the researcher is critical to designing good quality software. The software engineer needs to understand the technical domain to some degree, as well as the required function and behavior of the desired software implementation, to develop a cost-effective, user-friendly solution.

This document provides a structured approach to researchers, software engineers and project managers who comprise the team for developing a software application. It also serves as a roadmap for the software engineer to follow throughout the system development life cycle. If this approach is followed, the researchers and software engineer will be in basic agreement on the course of development from the onset of the project, which should help to minimize surprises late in the development life cycle and also help ensure that project milestones are met.

1.2   Purpose

This document provides guidelines to the software engineer for defining and organizing software development projects and to researchers for providing the necessary information to the software engineer for developing a successful software application. It serves two purposes: (1) it helps outline the System Development Life Cycle as it applies to building and building systems projects and (2) it enables the users to structure a software project based on this approach by using the included Requirements Template (Appendix A) as a guide. The template will help in developing the project plan and provide a structure for defining the requirements. By using the template as a guide when planning a software project, many of the critical elements necessary for developing the software will be defined. By documenting all the information that will impact the software development upfront, thorough, cost-effective software planning and design can be done with respect to the requirements.

1.3   Organization

The remainder of this document is organized into several chapters. Chapter 2 describes the phases of the System Development Life Cycle. Chapter 3 discusses how to implement a structured approach, and Chapter 4 concludes the paper. Appendix A contains a software requirements template, and Appendix B contains a project schedule template, both of which are recommended for use in any software development project. Appendix C contains a priority list template, which is used to establish priorities for project items. Appendix D is a case example illustrating application of the guidelines to a real-life software product supporting an economics project.

2   System Development Life Cycle (SDLC)

The System Development Life Cycle (SDLC) is a conceptual model for software development that consists of multiple phases: Software Concept; Analysis; Design; Coding and Debugging; System Integration and Testing; Implementation; and Maintenance and Support. Each phase can be thought of as a building block for the next phase. There are different SDLC models that may be followed, such as the classic "Waterfall Model," "Spiral," and "Evolutionary Prototyping," as well as many modified Waterfall models.[1] The key is to adapt a model that lends structure to your project. This paper features a Waterfall Model for the SDLC.

In the Waterfall model, a software development project progresses through a sequence of steps from initial software concept through maintenance and support. The model is sometimes referred to as document-driven because documents are produced in each phase and used in subsequent phases. The documents serve as a progress indicator throughout the life-cycle until a working software product is available. Planning is often difficult in software development projects due to intangible items. However, when using the Waterfall model the requirements are usually well-defined so planning can be done up front. The Waterfall model works well with complex projects where the requirements are well understood because the complexity can be dealt with in a structured way.

A fairly simple software project can become complicated very quickly, so keeping the project organized and documented is essential. Many projects fail or miss deadlines and come in severely over budget for the simple reason that thorough analysis and design are not done up front and risk is not managed. Careful consideration of each phase of the SDLC, while participating in a software development project, will greatly increase the chances of a successful project. Planning on several levels is essential for the successful completion of any software project. The SDLC can be beneficial to a software project regardless of the size or complexity of the project if a conceptual model is followed. The following seven SDLC phases illustrate the selected Waterfall Model.

2.1   Phase 1: Software Concept

The first phase in the SDLC identifies and defines the system to be developed. In this phase the researcher and software engineer brainstorm about the system and what it will do. Document requirements (using the template in Appendix A) as much as possible, so that an adequate system can be built that will be flexible for handling future enhancements. Communication among the research team including the software engineer, researcher, project manager (if other than the software engineer or researcher), stakeholders, and funding

---

[1] The "Spiral" model divides a software development project into several smaller projects that address the major risks first. "Evolutionary Prototyping" is a model in which a prototype is developed and eventually refined into the final software product. Hybrid SDLC models may be successfully utilized as well. S. McConnell, Rapid *Development Taming Wild Software Schedules* (Redmond, Washington: Microsoft Press, 1996), pp. 136-147.

sponsors is critical in this phase to ensure that proper requirements are obtained and documented.

2.2   Phase 2: Analysis

The team analyzes the requirements of the system to gain a clear understanding of what is required; in addition the software engineer must understand the technical aspects of the requirements. Figure out where and how the system will be used, who the users will be, and document everything for use in the Design phase. The team members must document even the seemingly trivial details gleaned during analysis, because these are the things that turn out to be very important for the proper execution of the software product.

2.3   Phase 3: Design

In the design phase, the analysis that was done in the previous phase is reviewed and the software engineer devises a design solution. The design must support the requirements and be as explicit as possible. Software design tends to start out relatively simple, but as all the requirements are considered, systems tend to become complex and unwieldy. It is good practice to prioritize the features based on importance and effort while putting together the design. Use Appendix B, a project schedule template, for documenting the tasks to implement the design. Use Appendix C, a priority list template, for establishing priority of project features. This way the coding schedule can incorporate the tasks associated with high priority features in a timely manner because there is the chance that items with lower priority may not make it into the software or may be included in a future release.

A solid architecture and design will avoid significant rework later on. Mainstream technology usually follows industry standards and is supported well; therefore problems can quickly be resolved when they arise. Careful consideration must be given before utilizing cutting edge technology. Since the technology is innovative, bugs and other technical issues will be present, and will need to be worked out as they are encountered. When problems arise, quick solutions are difficult to craft because the knowledge base and support is very limited. Even minor problems in these technologies can cause a cascade of modifications that need to be implemented which can adversely affect the whole project schedule and ultimately jeopardize the project.

Technical complexity increases the risk for the software project and should be avoided if possible. Issues resulting from unnecessary technical complexity can negatively impact the schedule, because a great deal of time could be spent trying to work around issues.

2.4   Phase 4: Coding and Debugging

Coding and debugging is the phase where the design is implemented by the software engineer. The design described in the previous phase serves as the blueprint for the system to be built, providing most of the information the software engineer will need. The software engineer will interpret the design and develop the code. Even when the software engineer is also the designer, it is important to have a detailed design, because it is easy to overlook minor details that can result in a major error.

Debugging is the process of locating and removing errors from the code. Most current programming languages allow compiling a "debug" version of the code. The "debug" version allows stepping through code, setting breakpoints, viewing current variable values, and offers debug information about the code that helps the software engineer locate problems. After the code is stable, the production version of the code is compiled and used for system testing.

2.5   Phase 5: System Integration and Testing

System integration occurs when distinct software modules are linked together and are capable of functioning as a unit. When there are multiple software engineers on a project, all the developers are expected to code to an accepted standard; if they do, and the design is good, there will likely be very few problems, if any, at this point. Unfortunately, this is not always the case. A common cause of system breakdown is a software engineer deciding that something needs to be done differently without informing the other software engineers. Because modules need to work together, a common protocol must be followed.

System testing helps to locate problems, and potential problems, with a software system. It is essential to have people other than the software engineers testing the software. It is a good idea to develop test plans to ensure that the testers adequately test critical functionality as well as less important items. For larger software projects, reporting bugs and prioritizing bug fixes will be a coordinated effort between the project manager, software engineer, and testers. Use Appendix C, a priority list template, for establishing priority of bug fixes. The software engineer and the project manager should come to an agreement on what to fix and what to let go, based on time, effort, and risk. This phase of the project usually takes on a life of its own, especially when the development team is large. In smaller software projects, testing tends to be straightforward, but in large projects, it is very time consuming to test every scenario, so adequate time must be allocated for testing in the schedule.

2.6   Phase 6: Implementation

Implementation is the process of installing the software on the customer's (e.g., other agency client, NIST Server) system and applying licensing agreements and access rights. This process can be somewhat difficult since it is hard to know exactly what kind of system hardware and supporting software may be encountered during the installation. As a result, problems occasionally arise due to compatibility issues. Prior planning can help to minimize some of these problems. Licensing and access rights that were established during the design phase will be applied in the implementation phase. Software may be designed so that certain features are limited or turned off based on the particular license that is applied. Appropriate licensing ensures the proper level of functionality for the software product. Proprietary libraries, dynamic link libraries (DLLs) and other modules to be used in conjunction with the software product being implemented are examples of entities that may require additional licensing.

After implementation, do a presentation for the sponsor and invite the sponsor to do some acceptance testing. Keep the sponsor in the loop during development so there will not be any big surprises at the final demonstration. After acceptance testing, and any final revisions following that meeting, present a formal letter to the sponsor transmitting the final product and indicating closure of the project. This meeting is a good opportunity to confirm the sponsor's interest in funding maintenance and support activities (see 2.7) as well as to identify the sponsor's interest in funding additional features suggested during testing (see 3.5.4.1).

2.7   Phase 7: Maintenance and Support

Maintenance includes items such as patches and data updates, while support includes bug fixes, help for users of the software, and collecting requests for new functionality. Discuss maintenance and support with the customer up front. Different types of maintenance and support may be provided based on what makes sense for the particular software product that is being created as well as on the needs of the customer. Determining the right mix of maintenance and support is challenging and fraught with uncertainty, but aligning customer expectations before maintenance and support issues arise will help maintain customer satisfaction and may potentially lead to additional future funding.

It is important to maintain a copy of the source code once the development effort has ended. It is also recommended to maintain version specific source code. There are a few different source control software packages that efficiently do this. Maintaining version specific source code enables an old version to be recompiled should unanticipated issues arise after software release. Depending on the agreement with the sponsor, updates for the software product may be issued occasionally. Data updates may be required, if requested by the sponsor, for software that needs to use a current data set. This should be contractually agreed to and not implied. It is important to maintain a copy of the source code, data, installation program and executable application in a secure manner after the project is completed. Maintain security by having the project manager and the software engineer keep archival copies.

3   Implementing the Waterfall Method for Planning and Executing a Software Project

This chapter provides implementation guidance for a software project. The main tasks found in a software development project are grouped by phase. These tasks are further broken down by responsible party: Researcher, Software Engineer, Project Manager, and joint tasks. Each software development project is unique and may require more tasks than what is listed here.

The SDLC outlined in Chapter 2 consists of the major steps for developing a software product. There are many different SDLC models, but what they have in common is that they provide a structured approach for developing software. Choose a model that best fits a project with regard to time, resources, risk and technical issues or follow the Waterfall model described in this paper. Planning the project based on a specific model helps to identify project tasks and milestones, as well as reveal timing issues that may not otherwise be evident. It is less likely that time allocations for major project tasks will be underestimated or omitted from the project plan when the structured approach is employed.

Identifying individual responsibilities (i.e., the researchers and software engineers) helps the two groups become a team by assigning individual ownership of certain aspects of the project. It also helps to visualize the general scheme of things so everybody has an understanding of who does what and in what order (see Figure 1).

Software Concept	Analysis	Design	Coding and Debugging	System Integration and Testing	Implementation	Maintenance and Support
Define purpose	Define user interface	Design software	Update the software project schedule	Review and compile comments from testing	Prepare media	Maintain version specific source code
Project proposal	Define algorithms	Provide feedback	Create application framework, operating modules and mathematical functions	Review software and assure that requirements have been met	Install software	Perform data updates
Define requirements	Define data storage and retrieval	Identify milestones and tasks	Write code and create the user interface	Prioritize comments into urgent, wish list or future version	Demonstrate software to sponsor	Maintain source code
	Specify domain rules and data variables	Develop software project schedule	Validate that algorithms produce correct results	Fix bugs resulting from testing	Formal letter to sponsor indicating closure	
	List assumptions and constraints	Provide required data	Develop draft documentation and/or help files	Finalize documentation and/or help files		
	Analyze requirements and document specifications	Provide test data and results	Compile debug and production versions of software	Peer review of software and documentation		
	Determine technology to be used	Provide technical text, terminology and abbreviations	Initiate alpha and beta testing			
			Arrange sponsor review			
			Create installation program			
			Develop marketing material			
Phase 1 ⇨	Phase 2 ⇨	Phase 3 ⇨	Phase 4 ⇨	Phase 5 ⇨	Phase 6 ⇨	Phase 7

   Researcher   Software Engineer   Project Manager   Jointly

Figure 1. Project Tasks Timeline

While many of the following tasks can be done jointly, identifying the party with primary responsibility helps avoid future misunderstandings among team members, and it is always a good idea to obtain input from the other party when needed.

3.1   Tasks to be Completed when developing the Software Concept

3.1.1   Researcher

3.1.1.1   Articulate the purpose of the intended software product.

3.1.1.2   Describe the level of user sophistication of the intended user group.

8

3.1.1.3   Present the software engineer with the project proposal showing milestones and due dates.

3.1.2 Jointly

3.1.2.1   Define the software requirements. Researcher and software engineer collaborate while defining the requirements to avoid items that may not be technically feasible.

3.2   Tasks to be Completed during Analysis

3.2.1 Researcher

3.2.1.1   Specify technical domain rules.
3.2.1.2   Specify key data variables.
3.2.1.3   Define the user interface features.
3.2.1.4   Define the algorithms to be used and provide brief descriptions of their purpose.
3.2.1.5   Define the data storage and retrieval requirements.
3.2.1.6   Summarize the research model for the programmer.
3.2.1.7   List all assumptions that are being made.
3.2.1.8   List all constraints that are evident.
3.2.1.9   Inform software developer if pertinent reference materials are available that may be helpful, such as technical reports and other software.

3.2.2 Software Engineer

3.2.2.1   Analyze the requirements to gain a clear understanding of the technical aspects, which become the foundation for the design. Document specifications of systems or subsystems, based on the requirements.
3.2.2.2   Determine technology to be used based on the requirements.

3.3   Tasks to be Completed during Design

3.3.1 Researcher

3.3.1.1   Provide required data in a format ready for use in the software product.
3.3.1.2   Provide a test data set and calculation-results for the developer to use to check the validity of algorithms in the software. An Excel spreadsheet may be created to define parameters and results for the calculations.
3.3.1.3   Provide timely feedback to software engineer.
3.3.1.4   Provide any technical text, terminology (e.g., glossary), and abbreviations (list of symbols) to be included in the software.

3.3.2 Software Engineer

    3.3.2.1   Design the software.

    3.3.2.2   Identify the programming milestones and break out the tasks that need to be completed by the software engineer and researcher to meet each milestone on schedule.

    3.3.2.3   Develop the tentative software project schedule to be consistent with the project milestones.

3.4 Tasks to be Completed during Coding and Debugging

3.4.1 Researcher

    3.4.1.1   Line up internal/external testers, initiate alpha and beta testing at appropriate times, and work with software engineer to incorporate helpful suggestions on a priority basis, as time and budget permit.

    3.4.1.2   Draft user documentation (e.g., help files and/or user's manual).

3.4.2 Software Engineer

    3.4.2.1   Update the software project schedule and identify target dates once the design phase is complete.

    3.4.2.2   Create application framework, operating modules and mathematical functions for the software product.

    3.4.2.3   Write code for the application and create the user interface.

    3.4.2.4   Compile debug and production versions of the code and test it for bugs and other errors.

    3.4.2.5   Validate that algorithms produce correct results based on data test set provided by the researcher.

    3.4.2.6   Create an installation program.

3.4.3 Project Manager

    3.4.3.1   Arrange for sponsor review and approval.

    3.4.3.2   Develop marketing material and plan for distribution.

3.5 Tasks to be Completed during System Integration and Testing

3.5.1 Researcher

    3.5.1.1   Review and compile comments resulting from testing.

    3.5.1.2   Review the functioning software product, communicate to software engineer any final changes needed in the program, and confirm that requirements have been met.

    3.5.1.3   Finalize documentation (e.g., help files and/or user's manual).

3.5.2   Software Engineer

   3.5.2.1   Review comments resulting from testing. Fix bugs that were discovered and make final enhancements where feasible.

3.5.3   Project Manager

   3.5.3.1   Submit the software and user guide for peer review. These may be reviewed separately or together. The project manager is responsible for overseeing the peer review process unless their manager designates an alternate.

3.5.4   Jointly

   3.5.4.1   Prioritize any comments from testing into items to be addressed with current funding and items to be included in a future version.

3.6   Tasks to be Completed during Implementation

3.6.3   Software Engineer

   3.6.3.1   Prepare the product (e.g., website and/or CD) for distribution and download.
   3.6.3.2   Install the software on the sponsor's hardware, assist sponsor with the setup, or host the software locally.

3.6.4   Project Manager

   3.6.4.1   Present a formal letter to the sponsor transmitting the final product and indicating closure of the project (i.e., the software is complete and functional).

3.6.5   Jointly

   3.6.5.1   Demonstrate software to sponsor.

3.7   Tasks to be Completed during Maintenance and Support

3.7.3   Software Engineer

   3.7.3.1   Perform data updates.
   3.7.3.2   Maintain version specific source code.

3.7.4 Jointly

3.7.4.1   Maintain source code. Project manager and software engineer keep archival copies.

4 Summary

This paper outlines a structured approach for developing software. The approach, known as the System Development Life Cycle (SDLC), provides a framework and direction for developing software from the concept phase to final completion. Following a structured approach helps to organize a project and put boundaries around a project that may otherwise become unwieldy. The SDLC defines seven phases that essentially are building blocks for completing the final project. The initial phase is developing the software concept, followed by, analysis, architecture, and design. Coding and debugging follows, which entail writing the program and debugging it. System integration and testing comes next, and then implementation follows. Finally, after the software is implemented locally, or at the customer's site, the maintenance and support phase begins. The SDLC can help to determine realistic time frames of a software project considering all phases of the project. Utilizing the structure provided by the SDLC in the software development project will facilitate communication between the researcher, software engineer, and project manager, thereby contributing to the optimization of development time, reduction of rework, and more productive teamwork.

Appendix A Requirements Template

(To be filled out by the project manager/researcher.)

Project Manager Name: _____ Target Completion Date: _____

Project Title: _____

Directions: Provide the requested information for each block in the template.
Background information: Include any pertinent background information. If this product is an existing software product, include its system requirements and why it is being revised.
Purpose: Provide a brief description of the purpose of the project. Describe the purpose of the software and why it is relevant.
Intended Audience: Who will use this product? What is their level of technical and software expertise?

Appendix A Requirements Template

(To be filled out by the project manager/researcher.)

Project Manager Name: _____   Target Completion Date: _____

Project Title: _____

Scope of the Software Development Effort:
This section identifies the boundaries for the project by documenting what will be included and what will not be included. While the purpose of the project generally defines the scope of the research project, careful consideration should be given in this section to specify the exact scope of the software, as it is often different from the project scope.

Identify what the product will do from beginning to end.

Identify the processes that will be utilized in the software product.

Identify the systems associated with the software product that will and will not be included in the scope.

Identify the organizations that will and will not be involved in the development of the software tool.

Constraints:
Include any limiting factors that will influence development. This could be anything such as a specific programming language to use, client-specific requirements, particular database to use, must be viewable on a pocket pc, etc.

1. constraint 1

2. constraint 2

3. constraint 3

Appendix A Requirements Template

(To be filled out by the project manager/researcher.)

Project Manager Name: _____   Target Completion Date: _____

Project Title: _____

Features:
Identify the features this product will provide. It may be helpful to think of each feature from the perspective of the user interacting with the software. Document the feature including any input from the user and the output from the software. If this is a rewrite of existing software or a conversion to a new platform, differing degrees of detail will be included. The objective of this section is to communicate to the developers which features need to be implemented in the software to help them to formulate a reasonable design based on the requirements.

1. feature 1

2. feature 2

3. feature 3

Algorithms:
Document the calculations that will be used in the product. Provide a formula and a brief description of what it does.

Appendix A Requirements Template
(To be filled out by the project manager/researcher.)

Project Manager Name: _____   Target Completion Date: _____

Project Title: _____

Technical Domain Rules:
Identify any technical domain rules that are to be implemented. The technical domain rules are rules that govern the internal decision flow for your proposed software. For example, a domain rule might state that *no tax is charged to customers with out of state addresses when purchasing online.*

Assumptions:
Define assumptions that are being made with regard to the software. For example, an assumption might state that *all single family homes in Maryland have basements.*

User Interface Details:
Document the user interface specifications. Provide any mock ups that may be available.

Appendix A Requirements Template
(To be filled out by the project manager/researcher.)

Project Manager Name: _____   Target Completion Date: _____

Project Title: _____

Database Structure/ Data Details: Describe the database structure, if existing. Describe the data set. Identify data storage and retrieval functionality, if applicable.
Research Model: Briefly describe the research model so that the software engineer can understand the basis of the software.
References: Provide references for documentation pertinent to this software such as technical reports, other software, etc.

Appendix B Project Schedule Template
(To be filled out by the project manager/researcher/software engineer working together.)

Project Title: _____   Date: _____

Directions: Initially, include each project task on a row in the template, and the item number. Add the planned start date, the estimated duration, planned finish date, resources required, and the task precursor item number. As the project progresses, add the actual start date and finish date, and check the item complete column when a task is finished.

Item #	Task	Estimated Duration (Days)	Start Date		Finish Date		Resource Required	Task Precursor Item #	Item Complete	Notes
			Planned	Actual	Planned	Actual				

Appendix C Priority List Template

Project Title: _____

Directions: Use this list template to establish priority for project items. Features, tasks, or bugs are examples of items that will be prioritized during the project. Provide the item name, designate the priority, and include any comments.

Item	Priority	Comments

Appendix D Requirements Template: Case Illustration

(To be filled out by the project manager/researcher.)

Project Manager Name: **Bobbie Lippiatt**   Target Completion Date: **09/09**

Project Title: **BusiBEES**

Directions: Provide the requested information for each block in the template.

Background information:
Include any pertinent background information. If this product is an existing software product, include its system requirements and why it is being revised.

BEES, is currently a PC-based software tool for selecting environmentally preferred, cost-effective building products. It is in widespread use across the building industry and beyond: there were about 24,000 downloaders of BEES 3.0 over the 5 years it was available, and we expect at least as many for BEES 4.0, which has been available since 5/07. A Google search for "NIST BEES" yields about 271,000 hits, and "BEES" is the search term most used by people brought to the BFRL website by external search engines.

BEES 4.0, runs on PCs with Windows 95 and beyond operating systems (see Vista note below) and with at least 60 MB of available disk space. A printer *must* be installed in order for the graphical results to display. Some people prefer BEES on a CD, so the Environmental Protection Agency (EPA) distributes on our behalf free BEES 4.0 CDs and printed manuals (even though the manual is already on the CD, some people like to see it in print). Vista: While we haven't been able to test BEES 4.0 on a Vista system, users tell us Microsoft no longer supports the WinHelp4-compiled BEES Help System. We've compiled Win2000-based help for one user who is currently testing it for us.

With this revision, we hope to transfer the tool to a web-based platform.

Drivers for revision:
- **While BEES Project Leader developed the software, her limited programming expertise—and programming language, Visual Objects 2.6—are both rapidly becoming obsolete and she does not expect to do extensive BEES programming herself in the future. With this platform move, we hope to use more professional, state-of-the-art programming techniques and transfer future programming tasks to a software engineer.**
- **Our largest user group is building designers, many of whom operate in Macintosh environments and who have requested a Mac version for many years. A web-based version would let Mac users use BEES**
- **We want the ability to post product data and documentation as they become available.**

Appendix D Requirements Template: Case Illustration
(To be filled out by the project manager/researcher.)

Project Manager Name: **Bobbie Lippiatt**   Target Completion Date: **09/09**

Project Title: **BusiBEES**

Purpose:
Provide a brief description of the purpose of the project. Describe the purpose of the software and why it is relevant.

"Green," or environmentally friendly, building is beginning to go mainstream and there is quite a bit of interest in measuring exactly what green means. Our BEES answers to "what's green" are widely respected because we use standard, science-based methods and because environmental issues can be quite controversial and NIST has a worldwide reputation for unbiased science. But the answer to "what's green" is, "it depends," so we need software to let users set key parameters so we can then develop results for them using our BEES model.

Our largest user group, building designers, consists primarily of architects—very "visual" people. They want us to deliver simple answers to the complicated question of what makes a product green. They would prefer a simple NIST-blessed list of "green" products to buy. By using our software, we try to gently educate them about the many criteria involved in assessing green, while at the same time not burdening them with so many choices that they are overwhelmed. Where possible, we provide default parameter settings. This user group is less likely to read our online help documentation and to "drill down" for detailed BEES results.

On the other hand, our BEES results can affect a manufacturer's bottom line, so this stakeholder group understandably demands that we provide detailed documentation on our assumptions for their products and deliver a high degree of transparency about how we score product performance. These people likely drill down for detailed BEES results and read the online help only about their own product group.

Over the last few years the BEES user group that has grown the fastest and today is nearly as large as designers is education, primarily at the college level. Many professors are using BEES in their engineering and design classes, and many students are using BEES in their PhD and Masters theses. We suspect that these users will be those most interested in the model documentation included in the BEES online help system.

We have BEES datasets for 230 building products in BEES 4.0. Some are generic building products, and some are brand-specific products. Designers want many more building products of both types to be included in future versions of BEES, but it is too expensive to add products in large numbers over short periods of time. For brand-specific products we rely on manufacturers to initiate contact with NIST and fund us for data development under our <u>BEES Please</u> program. These manufacturers would like to see their BEES results published as soon as they become available.

Appendix D Requirements Template: Case Illustration

(To be filled out by the project manager/researcher.)

Project Manager Name: **Bobbie Lippiatt**   Target Completion Date: **09/09**

Project Title: **BusiBEES**

Intended Audience:
Who will use this product? What is their level of technical and software expertise?

Following is the current distribution of BEES users by interest group:

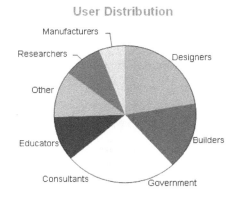

Their level of technical expertise varies wildly—from none at all to the Office of Applied Economics' (OAE) external technical peers. Even the manufacturing folks we routinely interact with have diverse backgrounds: from marketing folks to technical directors, from presidents of small family firms to researchers from multinational companies.

The level of software expertise among BEES users is average. We have discontinued extensive support for folks who seem to have never installed software on their own before. We also have noticed that the "average" level of software expertise and expectations have risen since BEES 1.0 was released in 1997, so we hope to adapt to state-of-the-art trends.

Appendix D Requirements Template: Case Illustration
(To be filled out by the project manager/researcher.)

Project Manager Name: **Bobbie Lippiatt**   Target Completion Date: **09/09**

Project Title: **BusiBEES**

Scope of the Software Development Effort:
This section identifies the boundaries for the project by documenting what will be included and what will not be included. While the purpose of the project generally defines the scope of the research project, careful consideration should be given in this section to specify the exact scope of the software, as it is often different from the project scope.

Identify what the software product will do from beginning to end.

The system to be redesigned begins with setting study parameters for evaluating the life-cycle environmental and economic performance of products and ends with performance results being generated for the user.

Identify the processes that will be utilized in the software product.

The product includes the working processes and subsystems required to evaluate product performance. The design, development, and deployment of the database are part of the project scope.

Identify the systems associated with the software product that will and will not be included in the scope.

The web environment, internet, and security are part of the project scope. Windows and Macintosh operating environments are not part of the project scope.

Identify the organizations that will and will not be involved in the development of the software tool.

The only organization involved in development of the tool is OAE. Organizations not involved include OAE contractors and manufacturers.

Constraints:
Include any limiting factors that will influence development. This could be anything such as a specific programming language to use, client-specific requirements, particular database to use, must be viewable on a pocket pc, etc.

1. **Code must be documented for long term use and the possibility that other software programmers may become involved in its development.**
2. **Must be platform independent**
3. **Must report results as multicolored graphs**
4. **Subcontractor delivers detailed BEES product data in Excel files (Note: Other formats may be possible as Excel is one of several formats for exporting their data from a commercial software package known as SimaPro 7.0; Project Manager has a copy)**

28

Appendix D Requirements Template: Case Illustration
(To be filled out by the project manager/researcher.)

Project Manager Name: **Bobbie Lippiatt**   Target Completion Date: **09/09**

Project Title: **BusiBEES**

Features:
Identify the features this product will provide. It may be helpful to think of each feature from the perspective of the user interacting with the software. Document the feature including any input from the user and the output from the software. If this is a rewrite of existing software or a conversion to a new platform, differing degrees of detail will be included. The objective of this section is to communicate to the developers which features need to be implemented in the software to help them to formulate a reasonable design based on the requirements.

- **Let user set two study parameters**
  - **Building Element for Comparison**
  - **Environmental Impact Category Weights: either BEES Stakeholder Panel Weights or Equal Weights**

- **Based on the two parameter settings above, report corresponding, pre-processed BEES 4.0 results saved as PDF files**
  - **Three summary graphs from 4.0**
  - **"All Tables in One" report from 4.0**

- **Let user print and save results**

- **Offer context-sensitive BEES help (extensive WinHelp-based help content already developed; can be compiled in other formats)**

- **Make BEES data files available for browsing (but not editing)**
  - **All BEES product files**
  - **LCCOST.DBF**
  - **EQUIV12.DBF**
  - **NORMALZE.DBF**
  - **WTS12.DBF**

- **Accommodate additional products as they become available without changing the software, requiring**
  - **Ability to replace existing PDF results files with new ones**
  - **Ability to add new building elements for comparison**
  - **Ability to add self-contained product documentation to help**
  - **Environmental vs. Economic Performance Weights can vary from 0 to 100 or 100 to 0**
  - **Discount Rate can be set to values between 0 % and 20 %, and will default to the current year's OMB rate supplied by Project Manager**
  - **Transportation Distance can be set to values ranging from 0 miles to 3,000 miles. (Note: algorithm accounting for transportation distance changes included in BEES code, but not included in Chapter 4 of the BEES 4.0 Technical Manual and Users Guide.)**

- **Offer more (≈5) Environmental Impact Category Weight sets to choose from, including a "no weighting" option and a user-defined choice (*can use Suit Selector code for the latter?*)**

Appendix D Requirements Template: Case Illustration
(To be filled out by the project manager/researcher.)

Project Manager Name: **Bobbie Lippiatt**   Target Completion Date: **09/09**

Project Title: **BusiBEES**

- **Offer more (≈5) Environmental Impact Category Weight sets to choose from, including a "no weighting" option and a user-defined choice.**

- **Enable Project Manager to readily edit help content**

- **Report both fixed, PDF-based results and real-time-generated results**

- **Retain BEES 4.0 PRODCOMP.DBF data structure enabling separate accounting for product components. (This ability is not now used, nor are there near-term plans for its use, but we don't want to rule it out over the long term.)**

Algorithms:
Document the calculations that will be used in the product. Provide a formula and a brief description of what it does.

The formulae and brief descriptions of the calculations that will be used in the product are given in Appendix A of the BEES 4.0 Technical Manual and User Guide available at http://www.bfrl.nist.gov/oae/publications/nistirs/7423.pdf .

Note: OAE has an Excel macro that confirms the BEES environmental performance results, so deployment of their complex algorithms in web application can be readily validated.

Technical Domain Rules:
Identify any technical domain rules that are to be implemented. The technical domain rules are rules that govern the internal decision flow for your proposed software. For example, a domain rule might state that *no tax is charged to customers with out of state addresses when purchasing online.*

- **For some products, a single environmental data file maps to more than one product**

- **Some Building Elements (Exterior Wall Finishes, Roof Coverings, and Wall/Ceiling Insulation) have additional parameter settings, data files, and computations associated with development of their BEES results**

Appendix D Requirements Template: Case Illustration
(To be filled out by the project manager/researcher.)

Project Manager Name: **Bobbie Lippiatt** Target Completion Date: **09/09**

Project Title: **BusiBEES**

<table>
<tr><td colspan="1"></td></tr>
<tr><td>

Assumptions:
Define assumptions that are being made with regard to the software. For example, an assumption might state that *all single family homes in Maryland have basements.*

- **The use phase for products, relevant for developing their data files and computing their life-cycle costs, is fixed at 50 years**

- **When letting user change default transportation distance for a product, we assume that product transportation is always the first transportation column in the product's environmental data file.**

User can enter study period length on a BEES comparison-by-comparison basis.
- **We will continue to evaluate all product alternatives included in a BEES comparison over the same study period, as required by life-cycle costing methods**
- **A flexible study period requires scaling of data in product environment data files**
- **A flexible study period requires making "N" in Appendix A, section A.2, of the BEES 4.0 Technical Manual and User Guide available at http://www.bfrl.nist.gov/oae/publications/nistirs/7423.pdf, a variable**

</td></tr>
<tr><td>

User Interface Details:
Document the user interface specifications. Provide any mock ups that may be available.

BEES 4.0 user interface displayed and documented in the BEES tutorial (Chapter 4 of BEES 4.0 Technical Manual and User Guide available at http://www.bfrl.nist.gov/oae/publications/nistirs/7423.pdf).

</td></tr>
</table>

Appendix D Requirements Template: Case Illustration

(To be filled out by the project manager/researcher.)

Project Manager Name: **Bobbie Lippiatt**　　　　Target Completion Date: **09/09**

Project Title: **BusiBEES**

Database Structure/ Data Details:
Describe the database structure, if existing. Describe the data set. Identify data storage and retrieval functionality, if applicable.

The BEES 4.0 database structure consists of 12 indexed data tables, as well as 3 tables for temporary storage of BEES results. Additionally, there will be a table containing environmental performance data for each product. For additional documentation, a "Brief Database Info" and a "Full Database Info" report can be generated for each table.

Tables with building product data; environmental files for 230 products: BLDGPROD, PRODCOMP, LCCOSTS, and UNIFRMT2

Files required for BEES result computation: EQUIV12, NORMALZE, and WTS12

Tables for the handful of products requiring use energy computation: BTUFLOW, USEECON, USEFLOWS, USEENVIR, and USEWALLS

Tables for temporary storage of BEES results: XTAB12, RSLTTAB, and RSLTGRH

For each BEES environmental performance data table structure:
- Note that the number of RAW, XPORT, USE, and WASTE columns can vary. Each product's column count for each of these life-cycle stages is given in BLDGPROD.DBF
- Note that the number of COMP columns can also vary. Each product's column count for the number of product components is given in PRODCOMP.DBF, by reference to this file's row count for each product

Data maintenance functionality
- Need ability to add, edit, and remove building products from the tool

Data storage functionality
- Two data files are used to temporarily store BEES results for graphical and tabular display by a graphing utility, but these files are emptied at the beginning of each BEES session

Data retrieval functionality
- Table 4.1, in Chapter 4 of BEES 4.0 Technical Manual and User Guide available at http://www.bfrl.nist.gov/oae/publications/nistirs/7423.pdf, shows the Environmental Data File names keyed to each BEES product, indicating files to be made available for browsing (no editing allowed)

Appendix D Requirements Template: Case Illustration
(To be filled out by the project manager/researcher.)

Project Manager Name: **Bobbie Lippiatt**   Target Completion Date: **09/09**

Project Title: **BusiBEES**

Research Model:
Briefly describe the research model so that the software engineer can understand the basis of the software.

BEES combines life-cycle cost (LCC) results for products with their environmental life-cycle assessment (LCA) results into the BEES Overall Performance Score, which helps building industry stakeholders, identify cost-effective green building product alternatives.

LCA--
Environmental life-cycle assessment is a "cradle-to-grave," systems approach for measuring environmental performance. The approach is based on the belief that all stages in the life of a product generate environmental impacts and must therefore be analyzed, including raw materials acquisition, product manufacture, transportation, installation, operation and maintenance, and ultimately recycling and waste management. An analysis that excludes any of these stages is limited because it ignores the full range of upstream and downstream impacts of stage-specific processes.

The strength of environmental life-cycle assessment is its comprehensive, multi-dimensional scope. Many green building claims and strategies are now based on a single life-cycle stage or a single environmental impact. A product is claimed to be green simply because it has recycled content, or accused of not being green because it emits volatile organic compounds (VOCs) during its installation and use. These single-attribute claims may be misleading because they ignore the possibility that other life-cycle stages, or other environmental impacts, may yield offsetting impacts. For example, the recycled content product may have a high embodied energy content, leading to fossil fuel depletion, global warming, and acid rain impacts during the raw materials acquisition, manufacturing, and transportation life-cycle stages. LCA thus broadens the environmental discussion by accounting for shifts of environmental problems from one life-cycle stage to another, or one environmental medium (land, air, water) to another. The benefit of the LCA approach is in implementing a trade-off analysis to achieve a genuine reduction in overall environmental impact, rather than a simple shift of impact.

The general LCA methodology involves four steps. The *goal and scope definition* step spells out the purpose of the study and its breadth and depth. The *inventory analysis* step identifies and quantifies the environmental inputs and outputs associated with a product over its entire life cycle. Environmental inputs include water, energy, land, and other resources; outputs include releases to air, land, and water. (*Note to programmer: BEES product data files contain their "inventories" of 504 input and output flows. The flows are the $I_{ij}s$ in Appendix A, section A.1, of the BEES 4.0 Technical Manual and User Guide available at http://www.bfrl.nist.gov/oae/publications/nistirs/7423.pdf). However, it is not these inputs and outputs, or inventory flows that are of primary interest. We are more interested in their consequences, or impacts on the environment. Thus, the next LCA step, impact assessment, characterizes these inventory flows in relation to a set of environmental impacts. For example, the impact assessment step might relate carbon dioxide emissions, a flow, to global warming, an impact.* (*Note to programmer: This is what the term IA_{jk} in Appendix A, section A.2, of the BEES 4.0 Technical Manual and User Guide available at http://www.bfrl.nist.gov/oae/publications/nistirs/7423.pdf does. The $IAfactor_i$ term is the multiplier for each I, and is given in the BEES file EQUIV12.DBF)* Finally, the *interpretation* step combines the environmental impacts in accordance with the goals of the LCA study. (*Note to programmer: This involves developing $IAScore_{jk}s$ based on environmental impact*

Appendix D Requirements Template: Case Illustration

(To be filled out by the project manager/researcher.)

Project Manager Name: **Bobbie Lippiatt**   Target Completion Date: **09/09**

Project Title: **BusiBEES**

---

category weight set (IVwt$_k$) chosen, then summing results to a single environmental performance score for the product, EnvScore$_j$.)

LCC— The LCC method sums over the study period all relevant costs associated with a product. Alternative products for the same function, say floor covering, can then be compared on the basis of their LCCs to determine which is the least cost means of fulfilling that function over the study period. Categories of cost typically include costs for purchase, installation, operation, maintenance, repair, and replacement. A negative cost item is the residual value. The residual value is the product value remaining at the end of the study period. In the BEES model, the residual value is computed by prorating the purchase and installation cost over the product life remaining beyond the 50-year period.

The LCC method accounts for the time value of money by using a discount rate to convert all future costs to their equivalent present value. (*Note to programmer: Refer to* Appendix A, section A.2, of the BEES 4.0 Technical Manual and User Guide available at http://www.bfrl.nist.gov/oae/publications/nistirs/7423.pdf *for the BEES LCC algorithm.*)

Overall—The BEES Overall Performance Score synthesizes the LCA and LCC results into a single score, as illustrated in Figure 2.7, in Chapter 2 of the BEES 4.0 Technical Manual and User Guide available at http://www.bfrl.nist.gov/oae/publications/nistirs/7423.pdf. Before combining the LCA and LCC results, each is placed on a common scale by dividing by the sum of corresponding scores across all alternatives under analysis. In effect, then, each performance score is rescaled in terms of its share of all scores, and is placed on the same, relative scale from 0 to 100. Then the two scores are combined into an overall score by weighting environmental and economic performance by their relative importance and taking a weighted average. (*Note to programmer: The formula for the overall score is given in* Appendix A, section A.3, of the BEES 4.0 Technical Manual and User Guide available at http://www.bfrl.nist.gov/oae/publications/nistirs/7423.pdf.) The BEES user specifies the relative importance weights used to combine environmental and economic performance scores.

References:
Provide references for documentation pertinent to this software such as technical reports, other software, etc.

BEES 4.0 and its technical manual/user guide (NISTIR 7423) are available for download from www.bfrl.nist.gov/oae/software/bees . (Note: BEES 4.0 online help includes all chapters of NISTIR 7423 except chapters 1 and 5. Help also includes Appendix B.)

References

Ferris, T. "Software User Assistance Project Management." May 21, 2007 http://www.klariti.com/technical-writing/TF-Software-User-Assistance-Project-Management.shtml.

Lippiatt, Barbara "Building for Environmental and Economic Sustainability Technical Manual and User Guide." NISTIR 7423. Gaithersburg, Maryland: National Institute of Standards and Technology, 2007.

McConnell, S. "Rapid Development Taming Wild Software Schedules." Redmond, Washington: Microsoft Press, 1996.